BASHABI FRASER was born in West Ben; [illegible]
two countries she loves most – India [illegible]
London, Bashabi returned to India to [illegible]
in the Himalayas where she was threatened with expulsion after breaking
all possible rules! Happily this threat never came to fruition and with a
PhD in English Literature she is now an associate lecturer in English
Literature for the Open University and a Post-doctoral Fellow at the
Centre for South Asian Studies at Edinburgh University. She travels wide-
ly both as a writer and academic and has written for many publications, has
two editions of poems in print and has been included in a number of
anthologies. Bashabi has also written children's stories and is writing a
shadow puppet play and a book on the Bengal Partition and is a classical
Indian dancer and choreographer. She now lives in Edinburgh with her
husband and daughter.

Also by Bashabi Fraser:

Topsy Turvy, a children's story (Dasgupta and Co., Kolkata, 2004)
JUST One Diwali Night, a children's story (Dasgupta and Co., Kolkata, 2004)
Ramayana, a shadow puppet play
(Edinburgh Puppet Workshop, Edinburgh, 2004)
Rainbow World: Poems from Many Cultures, ed. with Debjani Chatterjee,
a multi-cultural anthology (Hodder, London, 2003)
Geddes-Tagore Correspondence
(Edinburgh Review Book Series, Edinburgh, 2002)
With Best Wishes from Edinburgh, collected poems
(Writers Workshop, Calcutta, 2001)
Edinburgh: an Intimate City, ed. with Elaine Greig, an illustrated anthology
of contemporary poetry on Edinburgh
(The City of Edinburgh Council, Edinburgh, 2000)
Life, collected poems (Diehard Publishers, Edinburgh, 1997)
Peoples of Edinburgh: Our Multi-cultural City, ed. with Helen Clark and
Lorraine Dick (The City of Edinburgh Council, Edinburgh, 1996)

TARTAN
&
TURBAN

BASHABI FRASER

Luath Press Limited

EDINBURGH

www.luath.co.uk

First published 2004

The paper used in this book is recyclable. It is made from
low-chlorine pulps produced in a low-energy, low-emission manner
from renewable forests.

The publisher acknowledges subsidy from

 Scottish **Arts** Council

towards the publication of this volume.

Printed and bound by
DigiSource UK Ltd, Livingston

Typeset in 10.5 point Sabon by
S. Fairgrieve, Edinburgh 0131 658 1763

In memory of:

Thakuma: Snehalata Bhattacharya
Mum: Amy Fraser
Mejamashi: Niva Dasgupta
Sonamashi: Shanta Dasgupta
Auntie: Ellen Jay

Acknowledgements

Poems previously published as follows: 'Faceless and Free' in *The Eildon Tree*; 'The Bindi' and 'There are many things I can do for you' in *New Voices*; 'Mother', 'Waves' and 'The Familiar Figure' in *Markings*; 'To My Daughter' in *Poetry Scotland*; 'I am the ABSOLUTE' was composed for dancing for Scottish primary schools; 'Borders and Boundaries' in *Nomad, The Eildon Tree* and *Poets for Peace*; 'War' in *Nomad*; 'When will it end?' in *Bhinnochokh*; 'Benares' in *Poetry Society Journal*; 'The Gift of Water' in *After the Watergaw*; 'The Land of the Dragon' in *The Geography of a Himalayan Kingdom*; 'Do' care' in *Wish I Was Here* and the CD *The Jewel Box*; 'My Initiation to Racing Pigeons' and 'Dussehra on Calton Hill' in *Chapman*; 'Transformation by the North Sea' in *Poetry Scotland*; 'Between my Two Worlds' in *Wish I Was Here*; 'Ripples of Rhythms in Ullapool' and 'The Moving Image' in *Northwords*.

The Sikh Commemorative Tartan (worn by Gary Singh on the front cover of this book) was commissioned to mark the Jubilee Year of the Sikh community in Scotland, and also the Millennium and the 300th Anniversary of Khalsa.

Over the past fifty years the Sikhs in Scotland have contributed more and more to Scottish society. There are many historical links between Sikhs and Scots, with five of the Sikh regiments wearing the Campbell tartan, the sett of which has been used as the basis for the Sikh Commemorative Tartan.

The colours incorporated in the tartan are drawn from the flags of Scotland and India, and are bound together by the Sikh colours of tangerine orange and navy.

Contents

'Gifts Send Down Roots'
an introduction to Bashabi Fraser

THE NAME 'BASHABI FRASER' first came to my attention sometime in the mid 1990s when I was co-editing the *Edinburgh Review*. It sounded strangely familiar – Fraser was one of the surnames in my native village in Shetland, and 'Baabi' a familiar abbreviation for Barbara, a common first name there. By the time we met in 2000, at the launch of the pocketbook, *Wish I Was Here*, I had seen enough of her poetry to realise that here was an exotic Bengali flower, transplanted in auld Edina. On meeting her, it was apparent that she was no villager but rather a scholar from a great metropolis, a classical Indian dancer and cultural activist, drawing confidently on rich and ancient traditions – and that she had shuttled between Britain and India sufficiently for her to feel at home in Scotland, by the cold North Sea, writing in English.

In 1934 J. Leslie Mitchell[1] suggested that no matter how expert a Scottish writer becomes in the English language, there will always remain an element of strangeness in the writing which the true native English speaker will detect – with the effect of rendering the text in question as strange as that of Bashabi's great countryman, Rabindranath Tagore. The weaving of various new forms of 'English' out of local tongues and the Imperial standard in post-colonial times (which in Scotland owed much to Grassic Gibbon's own experiment) is a process that grids Scotland and India alike. The intervening years have brought appreciation of such 'strangeness' as a strength, and the muscularity of linguistic difference has flexed since. Poetry is after all, as the Russian Formalist 1910 definition of the Futurist poetic project claimed, very often a matter of making the familiar strange.

Bashabi Fraser's writing emerges from that fruitful territory between certainties and languages which cultural and geographical

---

[1] In the essay 'Literary Lights', *Scottish Scene* (with Hugh MacDiarmid)

removal entails, but appears at ease with this. She writes an English that communicates strangeness in the subtlest of manners, like a charming accent upon the familiar, spicing her vocabulary with words from afar as subject matter casts them up. But the strangeness is there too, in the way that the language dances out. Even as syllables accrete English meaning, underlying her work we sense there are other 'logics' that are essentially rhythmic and melodic – and essentially Indian. Sometimes, as if driven by a tabla player, the syllables dance quickly, keeping strict tempo; at others, swirling long lines suggest a classical Indian musician playing a raga, gathering key notes and improvising upon them, then returning to the silence of the margin and the white space.

Tartan & Turban focuses on clear themes and issues – displacement, removal, belonging, identity, war – but the abstract is not allowed to dominate. Poems throw up images both colourful and memorable, a kind of pageant of 'folk, work and place', celebrating difference while finding commonality. It reminds us that the links between Scotland and India, particularly Bengal, are complex and old, and that although there are many differences, we look to 'the same moon'. And it maps another kind of country too, that of woman, as daughter, bride, mother, outsider, victim and so on. There are urgent messages against war and repression, yet a faith that gentleness and kindness can prevail.

Bashabi Fraser's emergence confirms a developing sense of a new era in Scottish writing. This trend is also evidenced in the work of such varied individuals as Suhayl Saadi, Leila Aboulela, Sheila Puri, Irfan Merchant, and in a different way, Michel Faber. It is as if the generally urban and quintessentially Scottish writing of the early 1990s – in which 'internal exile' from the systems and culture of pre-devolution Britain found a variety of expressions[2] – has helped create the ground for if not inspire[3] a whole new wave of 'stranger' writing. But in this new era, neither protagonist nor

---

[2] Leonard, Kelman, Galloway, Kennedy, McLean, Welsh and Warner and the like

[3] The link in certain cases is acknowledged: Saadi has suggested it was the example of such as Kelman and Welsh that inspired him to deal with issues around his sense of alienation and identity, and to find ways of writing the language he heard around him.

author is fully 'of' the host culture in the way as was previously the case. It is work that offers a vital new view of Scottish life and questions the definition 'Scottish writer' itself. And when we consider 'new Scottish' writing such as David Nicol's *New Caledonia*, Alice Thompson's *Pharos* or James Robertson's *Joseph Knight*, or the geopoetic wanderings of such as Kenneth White and Gerrie Fellows, it appears as if some kind of internationalisation is taking place. 'Scottish' writers, broadly defined, are grappling with Scotland's relationship to the world. It is as if post-devolution Scottish culture is attempting to locate itself afresh, particularly with relation to its imperial past.

This 'new' Scotland is less self-congratulatory in the 'Wha's like us?' manner. It is more confidently self-critical, looking at the facts rather than the myths – consequently, realising its multiculturalism, it is a wee-rainbow-nation-in-embryo. At this moment in time, while the forces of the United States of America and Britain still brush the sand from their weapons, this comes as a comforting thought.

In her response to a passage from Khalil Gibran, 'Mine in Pain, Yours in Success', Bashabi Fraser writes that 'gifts send down roots'. *Tartan & Turban* is indeed a gift. I trust it will help her root still deeper in Scotia's soil. At the heart of this collection we find a great journey. It is a journey that has brought wisdom. There is a grace of reconciliation with dislocation and difference that others may draw solace from. We are all to some extent led elsewhere by life. These poems are, I feel, the expression of that common human desire to arrive somewhere, to give out the gifts we have brought and have them gladly accepted.

Robert Alan Jamieson

I

DAUGHTERS
OF THE
EAST

On a moonless night

There's a full moon today
But after ten long days
My grandmother says
She will fast
And why? – I ask.

Each year before
The cold winds blow
Behind a mysterious veil
Like a timid Hindu bride
The stars and moon hide.

Grandmother bends her head in prayer
And I wonder why
– Is it to have the moon up there
Exultant in the sky?

She fasts through many a weary day
And I have reasoned why
– Is it to chase the dark away
That rules her measured sky?

Come play with me ... it's HOLI![4]

Come play with me
   it's Holi!

Tell me you won't play
and I'll pelt you anyway
with colours that will stay
with you all day – for today
   is Holi!

You are the girl that didn't care
to throw a glance at me.
I am the boy that didn't dare
to ask you dance with me.

Today I'm out with my gang
drenched with colour, drunk with bhang[5]
I am your Krishna[6] come to play
your friends – my Gopis[7] who will spray
me with abir[8], for today
   is Holi!

And you my Radha cannot stay inside.
The spring sky calls, come play outside
with coloured water – do not hide –
for today ...
   is Holi!

---

[4] The festival of colour
[5] A drink made with milk, nuts and herbs, which is alcoholic and drunk on Holi
[6] The God of Love, who plays the flute enchantingly and wears peacock feathers on his crown
[7] The women friends of Radha, who is in love with Krishna, but shy to declare her love
[8] Coloured powder

Upset the coloured powder mounds
in clouds of purple, pink and green,
let your chunni[9] swirl around,
join your bangled hands with mine.

It's true I do not have a flute
or peacock feathers on my head;
I only know the Bombay hits[10]
and have a cricket cap instead,
which I will throw at your feet
and dance the bhangra[11] to the beat
as we sway our hips today
to the dholki's[12] frenzied beat ...

Rhythmic shoulders, clapping hands,
faces streaked, coloured strands,
saris sprayed, kurtas[13] stained
friends doused, strangers drained
from pistons, buckets, balconies,
street corners, terraces and trees –
till the wall you try to build
crumbles down against my will

I'll touch your cheeks and arms
with colour which disarms
you for one day
of abandon –
so let us play
as Radha-Krishna – for today
            is Holi!

---

[9] The scarf draped over the blouse and hair
[10] Bombay (or Mumbai as it is called) film songs
[11] Punjabi folk dance, danced by men to celebrate the harvest
[12] A drum
[13] Long shirt worn by men in India and Pakistan

SNAKE!

I

The cry was a signal to run,
after a split second to gauge its location
and then sprint in the opposite direction –
stretching the distance between it and me
till the ache of a hasty retreat
constricted my breath and my heart
weighed heavy in an effort to sustain.

II

Only Shiva[14] in his stony yogic seat
can relax with his eyes closed in tantric[15]
meditation and remain oblivious
of its power as it necklaces round
his neck and shoulders,
sidles up his erect still head
and fans out in crowning glory
over his artistic top notch –
spread out like a protective
umbrella over the head
of a dreaming emperor seated
on the snowy heights of Kailash[16] –
biding time – the destroyer
holding destruction at bay
as it watches and waits in a
stillness which reigns beneath
its mesmeric, awe-inspiring hooded gaze.

---

[14] Or Maheswar, is one of the Hindu Trinity, the Destroyer, who destroys a sinful
world, upon whose ashes Bramha, the Creator, creates a new world, which Vishnu,
the Preserver, preserves.
[15] Of the tantras, the religious texts of the Shakta cult
[16] The holy mountain on which the gods and goddesses reside

III

This Himalyan foothills jungle
has been appropriated and deforested
by a growing university campus of modern times
which pushed the elephant and the wolf back
to marginalized habitats and limited retreats,
leaving these beleaguered cobras to delve
in mouse borrows in these untamed fields
beneath foiled forests – now bared. They are
surprised out of their winter stupor.

IV

A new macadam road had been
rolled over stream, slush and grassland
marked out on a moonless night
by fluorescent lights, which we took
to assert our pioneering progress.
There was a group clustered round a
flashlight and following its beampath
I saw the proud hooded cobra,
meandering swiftly through the
primeval fields, to its doom,
held and led by the hypnotic charm
of a light, towards its waiting executioner.

V

The hypnosis was two-fold
and has remained so, as I have felt
its overpowering strength in its uplifted
curious alerted gaze – ready to strike
death, if threatened by destruction.

VI

Then the roads were all laid, establishing
human colonization of snake territory,
pushing through the remnants of a deciduous forest
we ventured through on dewy December
mornings – adventurous, enthusiastic joggers
plunging through mysterious mists
till we came upon the great convocation
stage in a cavernous auditorium
under a corrugated iron roof, but open
to the beauty of the backdrop of the Himalayas
in the north, lighted by the lilac of the dawn sun.
As we jogged into its shade, confronting
the stage on which we had unfolded
dance dramas, we were frozen into
statuefied awe as another dance drama
was being performed as the
night guard dozed in the audience stalls,
stretched on two chairs,
ignorant of the power spectacle
on stage. There was one cobra
coiled in dark dangerous loops,
its head held aloft as it watched
its two companions like a
king holding court from its throne.
Another lay sprawled in humble
homage at its feet, a huge
monster, brought to bow in full
subjugation. The third was a charged
bomb, now exploding in anger, fuming
and foaming as it riveted and
turned, whistling and hissing, swishing
round, speeding from wall to wall –
circling at lightning speed while
one watched with dangerous calm
and the other remained inert in
silent obeisance. We sprang into action –

nudged the sleeping guard awake,
pointed one warning finger at the
electrified stage, registering his
horrified recognition and then ran
with the urgent speed that picks up
with the fear of imminent danger,
unmoved by the promise of a vermilion
sky that had dispelled the early morning mists.

VII

While we welcomed the drenching
benediction of monsoon downpours,
we dreaded the floods that disturbed the
dry privacy of its burrowed home,
bringing it out onto our paths,
reminding us of a battle with the
wilderness that we had not quite won.

VIII

Having waited for a heavy
shower to soften to a drizzle
I had begun my journey back
on my bike, along the road that
skirted the forest, avoiding
its clustered existence, between
the Science buildings, till I braked
yards away from the covered
portico of the Physics Department,
surprised by the amorous intimacy
of two cobras, lying as if in
fulfilled exhaustion after a torrid union,
their black skins shining in purple blue
splendour under the white light of the
building entrance – a couple lazily
reclaiming the road we had built across

its territory, spanning the wide tarmac
like an Olympian boundary –
daring a brave sprinter to reach
their dual presence and claim victory.
I acknowledged defeat willingly
as I jumped off my bike, turned around
and took the wider, slower
circuitous road home, the King Cobras
imprinted on my mind forever,
to haunt my most restless dreams.

IX

Kalnag – the King of Cobras
who tried to overpower the God of Love –
Krishna – the dark one, turned
blue by the venom of Poothana's[17]
milk – immortalized and triumphant
and unconquerable as he danced
his childish dance of destruction
on its warring hooded expanse,
raised warningly above the waters –
stilling the deadly poison, willing
it to a crumbling submission till it was
lulled and tamed by the ethereal
notes of Gopal's[18] heavenly flute –
in the memorable Kaliadaman[19] –
the defeat of the King of Snakes.

X

So the itinerant entertainer
borrowing Krishna's gift,
has charmed its hypnotic deadly gaze
and willed it to sway to

---

[17] A demon who tried to poison Krishna by breastfeeding him with her poison
[18] Gopal is another name for young Krishna, the God of Love
[19] The vanquishing of Kalia, the King of Snakes

the snake-charmer's flute,
playful or angry, rhythmic and rippling
on city streets and village squares –
arrested from the primeval jungle
and smothered in woven baskets –
till it is allowed to emerge to
rock 'n' roll in the midst of an
awe-struck human circle.

XI

Its appearance and presence
have been accompanied by terror.
But I have never seen it strike
before we had struck it dead.
Stretching its slender neck, balanced
a few inches over my unwary mother's head
while she sat on a garden stool, while it enjoyed
the mild winter sun, perched
on her Japanese creeper encircling
her veranda with velvet purple flowers.
It has fought an unequal war
with our cat protecting her new litter
while it guarded the concrete platform
round our disused well.
But it always fell as my father aimed
at its pointed head, dealing its
death blow, seconds too late,
after my father had wrenched
its life out of its undulating body
while his heart lurched at draining
the life from its beautiful,
virile, delicate frame,
afraid as he was for his daughter
skipping home on unsuspecting feet
and trampling on one ready to strike.

XII

And when my unwilling daughter
in stubborn resistance, postponed
her eagerness to learn to balance
herself on her bike, it appeared
in her path – a lonely frightened
traveller from its lost underworld
to drive a freezing stream of fear
into her daymare, till she, in a bid
to survive, swerved round
from my balancing hand, to ride
unassisted, having learnt to cycle
home to safety from the reality
of the slithering presence of
A SNAKE!

. XIII

So now she can curl into a corner
and read about Nagini,
the willing slave of Voldemort,
striving to destroy Harry Potter.
She is smug in the knowledge that
Nagini, the Consort of Kalnag,
crawls through a fantasy universe,
unable to splinter through her
protected world of double glazing
in a country far away from
the Himalayan foothills she knew –
the lost territory of the
once-reigning Cobra,
the Monarch SNAKE!

Faceless and Free

When responsibility is transferred
From the perpetrator to the victim –
When the eye of the beholder
Is left free to rove, decry or esteem –
When respect is not possible to be decreed
As lust may follow a glance
Which does not see a face of compassion
Or the mind that might advance
His prospects, then he has to concede
That he needs to wrap his companion
Or guardian, his future dreams
Or disasters, so that he may remain the bastion
Of freedom or regard – his own
Against hers, *she* who is the devil
Of his desires, whom *he* can then protect
In purdah and revel.

Mine in pain, yours in success

after Khalil Gibran's 'The Prophet'
where the mother is told 'Your children are not your children...'

My children are mine and mine alone
The only gift I can claim as my own
As they are part of me, born of me.
Yes they do depart and roam free
Mingling their tears with the wide earth
Their sighs with the sky, their breath
Melting with gales that gather today
To lash tomorrow on lands far away.

And when they strike gold, the world is theirs –
Friends, family, renown and comfort declare
Their ownership of *my* precious gifts;
My gifts send down roots and branches uplift
To prove that my children have built tomorrow
And my body aches when they are in sorrow
And if they die, the world moves on
But they live in my heart, where they were born.

The Village Widow
to Jane

In my village, I am the widow
I went into mourning ten years ago.
Black is my colour, interrupted by the white
On my apron as I flit around the house,
Walk down the mountain road to the church,
To my neighbour's or the shop.

When I travelled north to see my grandchildren
In another country, my daughter-in-law said
I should colour my world in dress, scarf and shoes.
I saw mature ladies like me on bus trips,
Around coffee tables, shopping, laughing,
Wearing lipstick and confidence – living
As they had left death behind them
And weren't counting days till their own.
So I switched off my neighbours
And relations from my memory,
And for the moment became one of them.

The Bindi[20]

You can pick out my countrywoman
From an unrecognisable mass of faces
By that touch of colour on her forehead
That has marked her different from other races –

Of the world or of men in her own country
When they have owned or abandoned her;
And she has still flaunted it to hush up scandal
And has only wiped it off when they have branded her
Swathing her in sheets of white, leaving her arms bare
Her forehead – a testimony to death, a cleared parting in her hair.

But somehow, it never coloured my horizon
For my mother never used it
And I grew up not rebelling or repudiating –
Ignorant of the possibility that I could abuse it.
For me it held no semblance of reality
Till a spurt of nationalism forced on me its entity.

Then I matched it to my changing façade
Till marriage cut off all experiments
And limited me to that one unchanging flame
Scorching and unrelenting in the impediments

It set as a test to my endurance
Till I exploded from that latent heat
And was flung across continents
With the momentum of centuries of unacknowledged defeat.

But I had not won yet – for I disavowed it
Consciously, deliberately, till one day
A friend said, wear it as a birthright
And so I did, and do, though man's away.

---

[20] The coloured spot worn on the forehead to match the colour of the clothes Indian women wear

On the City Pavement:
A Metropolitan Mother

She sat on her haunches in her printed cotton sari
Its blushing hue echoing the young desires of her heart.
Her hopes leaped into the flames she coaxed
From the smouldering coals, whose darts
Caressed smooth cheeks. Her babe balanced
Himself gingerly against the wall
Of this colony of sackcloth which had sprawled
Along the pavement. As he blissfully relieved
Himself, she abandoned her fire and heaved
Him aside, undressing him with gentle hands
While he babbled with pleasure
In a language only she understood...
She sat his clean bottom on the dusty stone
And ran back to bring a lighted newssheet to burn
His waste. She wanted her world clean and germ-free
For her brood of five boys,
Playing and growing in their carefree
Open-air existence, surviving and thriving
Under the watchful care
Of this youthful metropolitan mother, striving
To give them a mouthful
And always there
For them – as the busy city moved on
From one cold night to another luckless dawn.

The Wedding Photograph

'Come to my son's wedding,' she had said.
'Can I take photos for our exhibition?' I had asked.
'Of course' she had laughingly complied.
So there I was seeing it all through a small lens
Capturing ladies in brilliant purples and reds
Defying the grey sky of a March morning –
Ladies holding lamps, lighting incense,
Settling chunnies[21], centring bindis,
Simpering, cajoling, flattering, tempting
The bashful groom with laddoos[22] and barfi[23],
While I trailed behind reams of yellow silk
That were gathered in a miraculous neatness
To frame his proud head in a turban.
Then the bagpipes drew me back to the streets
Where the white mare had come decked for
The brown sahib, and leading it, patting it,
Striding beside it were five handsome lads
Who turned round to me and said
'What about us? Won't you take a photo of us?'
I stumbled against the kerb as they lined up –
Five strapping cousins and brothers of the
Groom, in white shirts and green kilts, whom
I caught, confident and bold, as seconds before
One of them cheekily lifted his tartan –
His hand on its edge, shifted slightly, defiantly,
But frozen in time, framing tartan and turban
For the museum leaflets of a multi-cultural Britain.

---

[21] The scarf that is worn with a salwar and kameez or an Indian skirt and blouse.
[22] A round sweet made of ground lentils and sugar.
[23] A square shaped sweet whose basic ingredient is condensed milk, which can then have added items like carrots, pistachios, semolina, etc.

The Singh Twins[24]
'a box where sweets compacted lie'[25]

Inspecting this urgency of an individual identity
I have turned round to see myself mirrored in your face
My vision repeated in your dreams, my voice
Echoed in your speech rhythms, my pace matched
By your movements, my self-assertion mirrored
In your gracious acquiescence to absorb and renew
The world of our fathers, moulded by a mundane Merseyside…

Retracing the overland spice route, chasing the sun
To its source, to encounter it where it rises, suffusing the
Dawn waters of the Amritsar Temple and the
Agra Mausoleum, lovingly caressing in gentle
Light the Ajanta interiors and then flooding
A sub-continent, till its Persian past and Hindu
Reality blend and are vividly revealed in these
Inchscapes of intricate minutia.

They are modulated by the flood waters of Western masters,
But never submerged, as their delicate finesse demands
Attention which sweeping brush strokes cannot drown,
Catapulting the modern viewer into the hub of a
Sub-continental experience, moving beyond
A Degas-esque precision and detail into
An Asian interior of chaa[26] mornings, bhangra
Festivity and henna weddings, eastern barbecues, rhythms
Orchestrated by summer, memorable
Last suppers, snooker tables and snowmen in turbans
In this syncretic box where sweets compacted lie
Brought alive by enduring Camel paints, decorating
In figurative suggestiveness the dual consciousness
Of twin cultures, in frames too small to be invasive
Or threatening, yet vivid and candid in their reassertion
Of individuality, the recognition of multiple worlds.

---

[24] The Singh twin sisters had their exhibition of paintings at the National Museum of
Scotland, showing their British experience in paintings done in the Indian miniature style
[25] From George Herbert's poem entitled 'Vertue'
[26] Indian word for tea

Laproscopy

It was the prospect of a day off
Not ruled by alarm clocks and cereal
And driving against traffic at peak hour.
It was a day set aside from
Opening mail and working photocopiers,
Meetings, minutes and computers
– A day to walk across the Meadows before
Another summer day had begun for others;
To lie between sheets in the morning
And not feel guilty about reading a thriller –
To be talked to like a five year old
Appeased, reassured, humoured
– The centre of attention for a change.

But then the wind fell
And so did my sails –
I went limp.
Rendered semi-naked,
Punctured, prodded and devitalized –
Then brought back
To join a pack of prostrate
Dummies, all in shapeless backless gear
Motionless or stirring gently under sheets
That covered our respectability.

I was back to the clock
As consciousness ebbed and flowed.
I paid for it with hunger and thirst,
Pain and nausea and the reality
Of being a woman.

As I am Renewed Through You

The dreams of a golden voice
That I cherish and cannot know
The tunes that I cannot sing
I now sing through you.

The visions of movement
That I admire and cannot do
Of swift spins of freedom
I now do through you.

The tongues that I cannot speak
The words that I cannot know
The richness of understanding
I now gain through you.

The lands that I cannot see
The scenes that I cannot view
Of cultures and climates
I now view through you.

Of all that I didn't achieve
In changing society
Through dedicated service,
– I now leave to you.

Mother
to Rupa

From the moment the doctor passes the verdict
'Positive', her entire concentration now reverts
To herself, this time to a little form gaining shape, growing,
Breathing within her, for whom she becomes the pivot

Of existence, and the newcomer hers.
She watches those little hands and feet
She created, with tender wonder
And is willingly ruled by alternate yells and sweet

Toothless smiles that make demands on her
Attention, while her treasure makes progress
In turning over, pressing forward in an imaginary pool
And steadies itself against a chair and looks for a caress

When it falls backwards, before taking the first
Unsure step forward, which merges into a scramble
To move away from the one woman who was
The queen of its little world, which crumbles

In an imagination eager to outgrow the encumbrance
Of being indulged and advised, assisted and admonished.
So it breaks away to build new walls and new loves,
Feeling less tethered by old ties that were once cherished.

New-found confidence now polishes former uncertainties;
Happiness mounts and merges with social upgrading and promotion
With marriage and the circle turning a full round
When life is renewed with an unfathomable devotion

That is now transferred to a fresh pair of eyes
That hold one transfixed. And while they flourish
A personal despair reverts to one always there
To run to and feel the old feeling of being valued and cherished.

There are many things that I can do for you ...

There are many things that I can do
      For you.
I can bring the rain clouds from the south
And fill your April sky,
I can cool your burning forehead
      So damp.
I can break the silence of the night
And make the heavens tremble
I can moisten your parched tongue
      So dry.
There are many things that I can do
      For you.

When you're lonely by a seashore
Reclining on the sand
I can come in countless waves
      And tumble you.
I can swirl around your ears
I can curl you in my arms
There are many things that I can do
      For you.

When you rest a weary head on an outstretched arm
And stretch your arching legs beneath the table
      I can be a little myna
On your narrow window-sill
I can whistle soft and low till you are able
      To glance at me a while
To ease your heart and smile –
There are many things that I can do
      For you.

Daughters of the East

I am a daughter of the sun
I was born in the east
I have gathered in the forest
And laid out the feast

I have seen radiant summers
And felt my breasts burning
I have danced for the monsoons
With a deep urgent yearning

I have seen the snow melt
On the crest of soft dawns
And swell lazy streams
To urge them flow on

I have watched moving shadows
Of clouds on the green
Of paddy fields rustling
In a country serene

With stacks in the courtyards
And grain in the barn
And people going hungry
Most willing to earn

Breaking stones in the noon sun
With bangled arms
Plucking tea leaves in gardens
And husking on farms

Their colourful saris
Are bleached with the rain
As they sweat through long hours
And show their deep strain

On faces so tired
With thoughts for their young
Earth's daughters like me
Born to stay strong.

To my daughter

'Sylph-like' is what her proud grandmother calls her
As her gaze warms and envelops
A little girl growing between
One Easter and another Christmas
To a lissom adolescent.
She is my perfect ballet dancer
Poised and poignant –
Her feet on points
Her arms reaching upwards gracefully
Her look far away
Ready to whirl around and fly –
Be airborne and free.
Her small firm breasts
Nestling hopes and certainties
Of bridging the distance
Between the new roots
And old loves in
The land where the sun rises
To set dreams aglow.
  And so she grows –
  Her bells vibrating with a rhythm
  She weaves into her life,
  Combining the arrogance
  Of an old tradition
  With the anger of clattering heels
  In a new-found heartbeat
  That catches the
  Glittering colour of swirling skirts
  And merges with
  The fairy gossamer of tutu
  As eastern silk drapes
  Around western satin shoes
And my daughter
Unfurls her pretty petals
Wet with the dew of expectation
To combine her two worlds
In a freshly created pattern
Of movement and melody.

I am the ABSOLUTE
to the dancer in Rupsha from her mother

I am the ABSOLUTE
The One and Only God
I cannot be multiplied
Into several heads.
I cannot be divided
Into lesser Gods.
In me you will find
The Truth and the Word.

But as people of the world
– *You* six billion
Can view me as *you* please
In six thousand million

Forms. So if I am your
Creator, I am Bramha, who
Breathes you into existence,
Holding the Book of Life for you.

If you want me to
Preserve this world –
I am Vishnu who lies
On a lotus, as I whirl
The *chakra*, the wheel
Of Life in my hand.
And when you suffer –
Unable to understand

The violence and cruelty
Of a world gone crazy
I am Shiva, your
Maheshwar, who can raze
It all to the ground in a
Dance of destruction,
Circled by tongues of flames
My hand raised in benediction,
Which will reassure you
Of a better world
Created from my still centre
On the ashes of the old.
I am the same God –
The God of love and war
In your Kartik or your Krishna
Your fair God or your dark one
With the peacock or the cow
– As *you* choose to imagine me
I will appear to you now,
Willing your passion or your awe

Answering your wish or prayer
– I am always there for you
You goddess of learning and the arts
Your Saraswati through whom you pursue
Your love of reading, music or dance.

I am your gourmet God
Your mischievous Ganesh, your
Elephant God, whom Lord
Shiva calls 'son'. I will protect
Your business in adversity;
And my sister, Lakshmi with
Her grace, will bring prosperity

To your home. But when the
Demon in each one of you,
Rises up again and again
Against my might, I will subdue
Each demon – each *ashur*.

I will then be your Mother
Goddess, beautiful and angry too.
I will come as Durga
The mother of Lakshmi,
Saraswati, Kartik and Ganesh,
Riding on my lion
Powerful, just as you wish –
Bringing back peace to the world.

I stand at the centre, resolute,
Unwilling to multiply or be divided
Except in your dreams of the ABSOLUTE.

Borders and Boundaries

All over the world's white page
We create lines that are
Varied in their irregular pattern
Sprawling or angular, muted
Or sharpened by a desire
To demarcate the style between
One group of characters and
Another, to prove that we are
Different – central or peripheral
Having the right to rule or
The duty to defer, the Brahmins
And the Outcasts, the Enlightened
And the Savages, forever
Separate, guarding our territories
Like wary cats, our backs arched
Our eyes blinkered like horses
Our hooves marking the ground
Like bison, tethered to custom
Gnawing the ground, snarling, to convey
This is my plot, don't you dare enter it
Though I am ready to invade yours.

War

Rip up the flowers and ruin their hue
Bring blotting paper and soak up the dew
Pull down the curtain to blot out the sun
Stifle the wind and don't let it run.

Set the drums beating to frighten the sea
Watch it receding to eternity.
Send up your nets to capture the birds
Smother their songs, there's no time for words.

Paint the sky crimson with blood from the land
Gather the stars to splatter the strand.
Shoot your bazookas to break every string
Let pity and music fade on the wing.

An Abducted Woman
The Loot, a story from a civil war

She stands mute, her hands listless at her side
Her glance dead, her looks far away
Remembering each slaughtered head
Each torn breast, each splintered babe.
She still sees the venomous crowds –
Blood hungry wolf packs, carrying fire,
Setting fire, soaking living souls in fire
Till the flames encircle her and dance
Around her and in her and burn the light
Out of her eyes forever.

She is the booty the son has brought home
The last bargain thrown in the colossal loot.

Her red brown curls scorch the glance
Of his mother, her brown-green eyes
Quiver in their victim's domain;
Her golden berry skin tightens like
A taut, dry drum, over her keen-strung body –
Waiting to beat into a frenzy of feeling
Of fleeting feet and deer-like intensity.

'Look what I've brought home mother'
He gloats, 'a slave who will relieve
Your arduous tasks of fire and water.'
– Their eyes meet – of one beseeching,
Of the other searching. The silence
In the courtyard gathers in deeper folds
Than the one that settles
On mass graves of exterminated villages –
Till the mother decrees 'marry her first'
And the doe springs to life, crumpling at her feet
In the agony of having found refuge in one extant heart.

When will it end?
Caught in the Crossfire

I am eighty-six. I have seen life and lived it to the full.
I should die in my bed of old age
Closing my eyes with the consolation of leaving
Three generations to continue my dreams.
I have moved six times in eight days
From house to farmhouse, to a schoolhouse
Then a warehouse, to a shed, to a cart,
Which moves with me but none of my family –
I am the only one left of what was once a full house.

The horse that pulls us is worn
The wheels that grind along, groan
The land rolls by, forlorn
The sun darkens to mourn
– And I am weary.
When will this war end?

I cannot die in my bed
All whom I knew are dead
But when they allow me to die
Will there be a coffin for me to lie
In, on one small stretch of land
That I can call my own, and from
Which they cannot uproot me again?

This Land of Mine

This land is mine
for I was born here.
This land is yours
for you have
made it home.

And this earth
does not betray us
till we tear her apart
with shrapnel and shell.
Then she discards
her nurturing role
and rolls back her
green veneer to reveal
primeval rocks –
daring us to harness
her unyielding surface
and force her back
to bearing fruit again.
We have nothing left
between and around us –
this land, trust or a future.
The sky becomes
a passage of fear
the glint of steel
making us cower
where there is
no shelter left.

Then you and I start
an uncertain journey
driven by starvation,
desperation and a need
to carry on living
Somewhere ...

Refugees of the 21st Century

They come across a border
they have neither desired nor drawn.
Their bodies are ravaged by hunger,
their faces look utterly worn.

There was friction and fission around them
followed by famine and fear
And when home and hope were bulldozed
they had to seek comfort elsewhere.

So they come in a relentless flow
a trickle that swelled to a flood
The migration of a new century
waiting for a new God's Word.

Shadow Lines[27]

I am the daughter of the earth.
I was born to walk free
To traverse her expanse
To thrive in liberty.

She cast me forth as her own
To wade in her streams
To ford her great rivers
To set afloat dreams

Of plunging the ocean
To rock waves galore
That roll between continents
And break on new shores.

I dashed through green meadows
And conquered the slopes
I flung through deep forests
And nurtured great hopes

Of completing my journey
Where it had begun
Once I had circled and
Set with the sun;

But intangible shadow lines
Criss-crossed my path
And obstacles obdurate
Set aflame wrath

It was my body that they
Riddled with no trace of sorrow
Chopping and scattering it
With no thought of tomorrow

---

[27] Taken from the title of a novel by Amitav Ghosh

Waves

I have lain awake at the bottom of the sea
And when I slept, I was a somnambulist
Walking along the seabed, as restless
As the quivering, dark, cold world around me.

I have never slept in sweet repose
Never been lapped into a deep sleep
Of placid dreams of quietude.

But when I paced in a fever of cold terror
My eyes were shut and my brain
Awake to images that I saw
Only in the untouched recesses of myself.

One day I walked with my eyes open
And found myself floating upwards
In an impetus that sucked the waves
From beneath my propelling feet –

They fell behind and I heard them
Being suctioned back to the depths of past dungeons
While I stood flickering in the breeze –
A drop of dew, saved from a multitude
Dropped in the haven of
a broad green leaf of today's sunlight.

II

THE SAME SHELL

Sea Sound

Walking along the beach
I know that the sea
Is to be seen only and
Not felt by the swimmer
In me.

Last year, at such
A time like this
I was tumbling
Against the waves in Goa
In perfect bliss.

Looking across the
Horizon, I know
That the light will
Allow me to linger
More
Than I could have
On the other side
Last Summer in Goa
Where the crimson meant
That the sun would set
That hour.

Why, I wonder
Are my two worlds
So different?
A cold sea under a light sky
And a warm sea under a night sky –
One stops me at its brink
The other lets me dive and sink.

Absentmindedly I pick
Up a shell and for
A moment, lose track
Of where I am
– On which shore?

Is it the same shell
That lay on a Goan
Beach, and I had
Reached down and seen
Its fantail sheen?

It fits into the hollow
Of my hand
I hold it to my ear;
It makes me understand
That it carries
The same sea music
In its hollow
Which I had heard
In Goa.
And it has followed
Me here
The *same* deep
Churning wave
Sound that had
Curled round my sleep
There
Last summer.

Goa

It is my Bohemia
where a spring breeze blows in winter
making the palm fronds tremble with emotion;
where the sun does not burn
but shines with the caress of love;

where the sea awaits the expectant adventurer
and the shore stretches out to welcome her back;
where every hill holds promises
of curving arms to ensconce

and where, everywhere I turn
are the eyes, the smile, the arms of love
to curl, bask and build trust in

and live again.

Varanasi

Every brick wall speaks of history
Every paving stone echoes the past
The very walls mirror lives lived copiously
As memories wind through the memorable lanes
Weaving the past with the present
In a continuous stream of pilgrims paying homage ...

They come to this holy city
Where temple and palace
Guest house and alm-house
Stand shoulder to shoulder,
Walking down the ancient lanes
Stopping by the life giving river ...

It is holy in the halo that lingers over
Its stone steps, where sins are washed away
By the water lapping at the edge
Of a musing populace of ancient edifices.

It is sacred as all is sacred –
Human life, animal life,
Motherhood and old age
Relationships and society –
Vegetation, procreation and death.

Life and death meet here
From the first spark of dawn
With ablutions and cremations,
Lit by the rosy tint of the same sun
Which begins and ends each day –
Shimmering on its edge

Warming and flushing its very depths
As it receives the tired prayers and pains,
Cleansing and washing the living,
Taking the remains of the dead away –
While the Ganga assures Varanasi of continuity.

Dawn on Tiger Hill

From Darjeeling it is a breathtaking climb
Swaying round dizzy bends as the road
Leads one round in an eightsome reel
Through the wee small hours in an old Ford.

The houses silently clutch the slopes of the town
We leave behind, asleep and watched over by the strange
Shapes of dark pines on a cold summer night,
Splintered by stars which spill over the next range.

The Ford joins a battalion of old jeeps short of the crest
Of the sleeping tiger. We strain forward –
As part of a tremulously expectant tide
Which advances towards

The source of first light, as it is displayed in
Vibrant chords played on those vast snow-clad peaks
As if one powerful artist had burst the dam of a channel
And let the colours of the rainbow sweep across in streaks

As stroke after stroke of tinted shadow breaks and shudders
Over the expanse of the Kanchenjunga[28] –
The colours repeated like notes in succession on the clouds
That lie in feathery sheets below us like a misty Ganga[29]

Violet, mauve, lilac, pink, peach, golden and vermilion –
The strokes ascending and descending, initiated
Behind the range, reflected across the sky, on the mountain,
Down on the clouds and back again, till it is reiterated

In the human tide which has gathered
Momentum and held its breath until it attains
The climax. And the Himalayas reverberate with the symphony
Of an applause greeting the sun, as it subsumes the colours and reigns.

---

[28] Kanchenjunga: a Himalayan peak, the third highest peak in the world, which is always snow-capped

[29] Ganga: the Indian name for what is known in the west as the river Ganges

The ballot box explodes
Rajiv Gandhi's assassination

A meteoric flight
Splintered as it beamed in delight
On a people's favour.

Such is India –
It holds us there
In a primeval past.

We may talk of a break
Put all we have at stake
To ensure a revolution.

So we welcome a renascence
Look towards a transcendence
But all is lost in a flame.

Non-violence becomes a dream
In this oozing, bloody stream
That is released.

There's a chance for everyone
As today's Indian
To remain in obscurity and live.

But if one dares the sun
In a run to change all –
He is done.

The ballot box explodes
In bullet episodes.
If India wins, she will have won
With a sum
Paid in terms

Of human lives
That are cheaper today
Than they were yesterday
And the price goes down
With the sun.

A Colossal Dignity

I have seen you walking through the forests of India
A being that has been able to endear
Itself to kings and countrymen, soldiers and farmers
The symbol of India's size, age and dignity in harness.

I have watched you as you stopped by a stream
Dipping your trunk in lazily as you gazed
In the distance, then spurting your unwary companion
With water, as he stood unsuspecting and amazed.

I have marvelled at your concern as you stepped gingerly
Through village streets and busy roads
Conscious of your great weight and strength
As you laboured under heavy loads.

I have come across you in a mood of abandon
Playing football with barrels and crates
Splashing colour as in Holi, or drunk
On country spirits as you romped with your mates.

Your memory confounds, your intelligence prevails;
But have we paid the homage that is due you –
A companion fit for mystics and monarchs,
A considerate mother – and a friend so true?

Piu – where are you?

What is that I heard –
Was it a bird
Shattering the night?

There it goes again
A plaintive refrain
Crying out of sight.

Why do you weep
When I want to sleep
Piercing the silence?

I hear you search
From your hidden perch
In a voice so intense

Saying 'where are you?'
To your friend Piu
In a heart-rending cry

That ascends in degrees
Till it rocks the trees
And vibrates in the sky

Oh if I had known
Where your Piu had flown
I'd bring her to you

To cradle and guard
You from any hazard
For my peace and yours with Piu.

A Tornado on the East Coast

There never is enough time –
Tripping up every minute
To make the round of closed windows
Pick up the book I forgot
Steer my eldest – backpacked
And rearing, and wheel the stroller
To the door – when the brilliant
Morning is blotted out like a
Projector screen between one slide and
Another and my backyard window
Is shadowed by a spiralling
Darkness – a demon's heaving breast
That tears the front door open
And a compelling wind swirls through
This ranch house. And my daughter?
Has she been sucked up by this
Demonic visitation? And my little one?
I rush back to her crib –
She lies alert and expectant
Holding out her little hands as
My eldest returns her soft chipmunk
Which she had dropped seconds
Before my neighbour's deck
Was neatly wrenched and gracefully swung
Over my roof, to be relocated
In my front-yard before this
Capricious phenomenon sought another site
To engage its torrential attention
While silence returned to this
Provincial street of ours and
We picked up our pieces, grateful
That our ranch house was still standing
Till the next unprecedented tornado descended.

Upheaval

A boat upturned, a flood returned
A watershed to drown the bed
A storm to break the placid lake
A tide to bend a river's trend
A cyclone's rage to cause outrage
An ocean churned, existence spurned
A fury hurled to drown the world.

From a Temperate Spring
to a Tropical Drought

I turn from this longing for the sun
This euphoria when it shines
This ecstasy when its heat
Warms me and this country, and turn
To the knowledge that confines
My gladness and my heart beats
For those vast plains that burn
Through years, forsaken by the rains
As life in its cyclic persistence
Has compelled scorching hands
To fell trees and rob the terrain
To fuel life, in its resistance
To be cowered in a land
Of millions, nurturing hope amidst pain.

The Gift of Water[30]

There is a beautiful girl in a cave
Where I can hear her weep
Singing sad tunes that ripple the wave
As she sighs herself to sleep.

She weeps for her land
She weeps for her love
She weeps to be free and run
She looks for a hand
To stretch from above
And open her cave to the sun.

The wave runs into wave to set
The youthful stream a-flow
Which has been born of tears spent
In darkness and in woe.

Till one day she turns around to face
The awning so long barred
And climbs the rock to greet the space
Where her stream flows undeterred.

The stream now gathers grace and strength
To widen bank and bed
To create springs and lochs of length
In lonely glens, that know instead
Of tears, they now can bring
The gift of water from her being
Free to live and free to love
And free to wed the sun above.

---

[30] From a combination of Celtic and other myths, where a girl sits imprisoned. Her tears create a stream and her sighs, the wind. One day she realises that she needs to will her own freedom, and once she is free, the stream of tears becomes the life-giving gift of water, as the girl – the symbol of fertility – is wed to the sun.

There will always be ...

There will always be
Paddy green for me
Though the floods come every year
And flow relentlessly.

There will always be
Mango groves for me
Though the storms come to shake
And break the buds from trees.

There will always be
The palash[11] and sheuli[12]
Of flaming red and dewy white
Against the sky, blown on the grass
– But blooming profusely.

---

[11] The palash tree has red, flaming flowers that bloom in March/April when the sun is very hot in a clear blue sky. The Battle of Plassey (won by Clive in Bengal against Siraj-ud-daulla, Nawab of Bengal, in 1757), or 'Palashi' as one would say in Bengal, took place in what must have once been a field of palash trees.

[12] A white flower with single petals, an orange stem and a sweet perfume, which blooms in September/October. The flowers are found early in the morning on the ground, shed by this delicate tree, from where they are picked and made into garlands.

The Land of the Dragon (Bhutan)

In the land of the dragon, the dzongs[33]
Have stood the Himalayan storms
Of elemental existence, carrying in
Their holy recesses, the silent norms

Of an old recluse's culture
Held within the silken folds
Of Buddhist texts, lit with
A hundred lamps, which hold

The key to the secret of its strength
In fortitude, a nation closed
Till of late, to the doors of the world
Waiting for the dragon who dozed,
To awake and let the shadows from across
The ranges roll over the Bumthang valley
Marvelling at the open countryside that was,
Till forty years ago, inaccessible, till
A frolicsome road looped round the bends,
Brazenly staring at Tangsibi[34] from the hill,
Invading Ura La Pass, to ring the bell
With impish glee at its chorten[35]
Breaking the sanctity of Gankar Punsum[36]
– Devouring its virgin beauty with a wanton
Appetite, till the road came to rest
In Ura village, creeping with docility through time
Into the new temple to Guru Rimpoche
Willing to wait –
Unwilling to startle the dragon in a fresh climb.

---

[33] Buddhist monasteries
[34] a village
[35] a shrine holding a saint's relics
[36] Bhutan's highest peak

In a Buddhist Monastery

I took my shoes off at the entrance
Leaving the dust of another world behind.
I carried the peace of the silent mountains closing in
Ringing in the intruder to part the curtains of the past
And enter a world forgotten by the world at large.

This was the haven recluses chose to meditate in,
To live stark lives unhampered by desire;
The darkness lit by a myriad gentle lamps
Reflecting the certainty of the Enlightened One.

I stood in awe in the presence of the Compassionate
A calmness entering my searching self
Humbled by the library of silk scrolls
Which held the tenets of a way
That eluded me and lay beyond the reach of restless souls.

The Great Divider

If faith in God divides
The human race,
If love of the Maker
Is cause for distress –
If hate is synonymous
With religion –
Then let me live in doubt
And isolation,
Free from shells and mortar
Sword and knife,
And turn away from fear
That overshadows life

The Same Moon:
from Edinburgh to Calcutta
a refracted lens

And what do you discern
When you turn your gaze
From the crystal lights
Of February nights
To return to the dewy days
Of eastern ways?

You are startled by the heron
That you mistake for a gull
As it stilts across the Maidan[37]
Which hasn't seen the fall
That has cast in winter shadows
The verdure of your Meadows.

You wonder how would Outram
Have responded to Gandhi's March
If they had met out on his ghats[38]–
Could such a meeting build an arch
Across the Hoogly – stall the dam
That rose between it and the ramparts

Of Empire? You stroll in dreamy reverie
Recollecting clouds of snow
That clustered round your feathery glow
Jolted by the jagged line
Of towers towering your skyline
So used to Georgian revelry

---

[37] Meadows in the heart of Calcutta
[38] Outram Ghat: The jetty named after Lord Outram, on the river Hoogly at
Calcutta

In granite, masoned to portray
A stolid Highland holding sway
Only to be outdone by hills
That gently push their way
To breathe free and softly feel
Your silvery light, that now
Has skirted the dark brow

Of Arthur's Seat, to encounter the numerous halls
Of the Governor's Palace and its walls
Gleaming, as you race to face
The Gothic splendour of the days
Of High Court's rule. Then it's a leisurely stroll
Round Dalhousie's[39] empty mall
Wondering at the red brick walls
Of Writers' Building[40], reminiscent
of your British days.

---

[39] A square in Calcutta, named after Lord Dalhousie, with buildings from the Raj
[40] Office of the West Bengal State Government, built as the seat of the Government
of the Raj

The World at the Doorstep

What makes a city welcoming and intimate
When can it seem distant and indifferent?
When do its stone walls speak with nostalgic garrulity
When do they freeze to a coldness of chilling brutality?

Was a city born a city, or did it gradually grow
From house clusters, to strings of streets, to a metro
Submerging hamlets which merged with its own
Expanding a skyline that flung its net wide
To capture an urbanscape and stop with the tide?

A city is not of buildings alone
But of people who linger and make it their home ...

As the world changed frontiers
And Empires gave way
People returned with old memories
Of lands they held sway
Over centuries, and a generation
Which once ruled the world
Could not but wonder
At how things had turned.

Is this then a city that they left to roam
Beyond this cold island, across the deep foam?

They came back to witness a city that had spilled
Over borders they neither recognised nor willed.
This world at their doorstep they now have to share
And welcome because they had once been there.

III

TARTAN
AND
TURBAN

Do' care

In a Paris hotel lounge on one occasion
My thirteen-year-old five-foot-five
Daughter glowed with the attention
Of three young men striving
To pigeon-hole her Scottishness
And break her brittle brusqueness
With their far-eastern finesse.

If Scotland played England
Whom would she support
– Sco'land – was the answer delivered
And if England played India
– India – she claimed with triumphant swagger.
If England played Germany
– Germany – was the response
From the unassailable position
Of a new-found nationalism.

And what if it were Scotland and India
One demanded with the diabolical confidence
Of an argument-winning lawyer –
She clamped down her glass, shrugged her bare
Shoulders, turned away saying – do' care.

Tartan & Turban

Give me your tartan
And I will imbue it with
The spirit of my race.
I can defend your borders
As I did the Punjab's
In long war-torn days.

I will wear your tartan
With the pride and strength
Of my history and tribe.
I will weave in its pattern
The breadth and length
Of five rivers that subscribed
To my wealth, which I will now
Lend to your tartan
And make it mine – this new
Singh tartan, willing to
Blend with my Sikh turban
At my journey's end.

Paisley

Paisley on your palate
And paisley on your looms
Paisley round your shoulders
And paisley in your rooms
Paisley softening cushions
Paisley brightening rugs
Paisley lacing tables
And ornamenting jugs

Brought from the Kashmir valley
This curious mango shape
Chained out in complex colours
And designs for your landscape.

An Intimate City

The hazy glow of yellow festooned lights
Above the edge of the gentle slope
Of Bruntsfield Links, flanked by the stately
Steeple of what is no longer a church,
Was my first glimpse of Edinburgh.

This intimate city, which I could walk across
And not miss a car; where I did not have to
Queue through lunch breaks to see Royal Shakespeare
Or sway in a tube for two hours to crash into an Albert Hall.

Its Georgian grandeur and Victorian vanity
Make it a citadel of time, defying change.

Skyscrapers have marred its peripheral skyline –
But the straining streets reminding me of Darjeeling
Its spectacular castle at the summit of its hilly centre
The palace in the Park and Princes Street where people meet
Remain as the throbbing heartline of an urbanscape
Caressed by the sea and watered by the Leith,
Cradled by the Forth and guarded
By the lion which crouches at its masthead
Bidding all the other beasts of Blackford and Braid
                        to kneel and ponder
On this city of green Meadows and stone streets –

Seat of monarchs and poets of all times
And politicians and citizens hopeful of tomorrow.

Two Colonies

I

Looking out across the skyline
From the high point of a studio hall,
My gaze did not skim the tenements
Or flash across the hills beyond...
But dropped a few feet below
To spy on and eavesdrop
On the home life and family secrets
Of a colony of seagulls who had built
Their estate of identical bungalows –
Top open and crowded together
And bustling with comings and goings
With greetings and goodbyes
With mealtimes and bedtimes
With skirmishes and bonding
In diverse families with varied habits.

II

This whole new world of self-absorbed activity
Came as a total but welcome surprise
And I was able to accept it as
I had been prepared years earlier
When we had made a deliberate trip
To a bird sanctuary of migratory flocks
In a tropical habitat, where we climbed
The watchtower in the crimson light of the
Setting sun, and looking down on trees below,
Took minutes to realise that those flamboyant
Pink flowers, which looked like gigantic
Orchids, were not of the tree at all
But hundreds of flamingos which dominated
The green leaves and brown branches
– Breeding and feeding and tending
Their young, raising a cacophony
Of sounds of a busy settlement
– But the difference was that while
That was like a modern film
This scene was like watching
A silent 50s film in black and white,
Guessing at the conversations
And quarrels, the love tales and stories
– All imagined through the soundproof,
See-through wall of double-glazed windows!

My initiation to Racing Pigeons
to Stephen

I was allowed to fill the narrow corn troughs
By this hulking, reticent neighbour of ours
Who had the absurd Biblical name of Barnabus.

My full initiation came on one long warm July
When Barnabus called me aside and said he could rely
On me to take charge of his brood – to check their supply

Of food and water, of their flights and returns.
In that amazing, idyllic summer, I was able to discern
Each bird's peculiarity and in that intimate sharing, learn

Of courtship and love, of a female's sharp wrath
If wooed out of time. Of the beauty of birth,
Of regurgitation, growth and unexpected death –

Which came as a shock, when the fairest archangel
Came reeling back in the first stage
Of my apprenticeship – and I confronted old age.

Priesthood came with Barnabus' return, bringing greater rewards
As he presided over the registration of the ring, and I looked forward
To a fledgling's vow to dare. At first it turned back towards

Barnabus and my youthful captivity
To this sport – a mutual susceptibility –
Indistinguishable in each shared activity.

So Barnabus taught me the final test of weaning,
When a bird could pick up corn from the floor, learning
Like its mother, to peck and choose. And my old man discerning

My obsession, made me the dream gift
On my tenth birthday – a real pigeon loft,
Converting our old caravan by his imaginative craft

To house my first tired tippler, whom I acquired
From my Guru for 3 bob, which I had paid
With pride. The next was a tumbler, dearer but worth the quid.

… Soon I had them all, dove grey and dark slate,
Speckled and blue tinged, their fragile fate
Bound close to mine. I could remember each date –

When I bought them or found them, full-grown
Or new born, injured or lost, discarded or torn
From the flock by fatigue; and they thrived on my corn.

My greatest joy was when one evening
Barnabus hid my slight, nervous frame under his wing
Of an overcoat and took me into the sanctum ring

Of his Racing Club cronies, whose pretence
Of not noticing my underage presence
Became for me their mark of acceptance

Of my pigeon racing days, which then, didn't seem in vain.
So we ventured, taking our pigeons in Barnabus' Volkswagen
To challenge our flying emissaries with ardour,
                              willing them to return again.

Nothing had prepared me for the snow

I had heard the thunder in the night
And seen the lightning flash
I'd felt the monsoons drenching might
And knew that trees would crash.

I was prepared for city streets
To be transformed overnight
So that I could then retreat
To the garden in delight.

But all the stories I had heard
And all I thought I knew
Had not really prepared me
To visualize the snow.

It did not slash down like the rain
It did not flow in streams
It came without me knowing when
And made the whole world seem

A dream in white
Of which I'd write
To granny far away ...
But what would I have to say?

Transformation by the North Sea

The wind raced across from the North Sea
Through the Meadows to awaken me
To the reality
Of this stormy city.

It unfurled the folds of my sari
Till it billowed out in outraged fury
And I vowed I'd reject its gracious dignity
Till I was in a climate of predictability.

So I have swathed my femininity in denims and coat
My tresses held back by a tea-cosy hat
In a crowd I know that I always stand out
In spite of my accent and tartaned format!

The Surprise Wedding

She picked up her white wedding dress and gathered
Her trail in her hands and on invisible wings
She lifted her being over the North Sea's forbidding surface
In a determination to have her wedding elsewhere. She soared –
Carrying her ethereal muslin folds which caressed the engulfing air
And smothered in billowing, feathered nothingness
The Firth of Forth's stretching arm, kissing the face
Of the lion guarding Edinburgh, from where
She took stock as she paused in her flight ...

And then in a sense of happy abandon
She swirls over the city, letting her gossamer dress drown
Its vision, blowing her dewy kisses as she alights
From above its Georgian building, to its peopled streets,
Draping wynd and close as her muffled wedding march
Picks up its pace and in one wild ecstatic moment
She finds her heavenly host welcoming her here
On the hills and Parks and in quiet retreats –
They scatter confetti which mingles in this eccentric search
For a venue for the bride's wedding, whose excitement
Is translated to us in the moist embracing softness of a haar.

The Familiar Figure

On summer mornings, when the Royal Mile
Was enlivened by the enthusiasm and exclamations
Of camera loaded tourists, I have seen him
Trudging up from where the Palace stands –
With four plastic bags, worn with time and grime
Full of his prized possessions, his face impassive
To his surroundings, living with his memories
And now holding their remnants in those four plastic bags.

Where did he dream the night away of happier days
Why was he always walking uphill in the mornings
What did he guard, clutch at and carry
So jealously? Where was he going?

He never glanced up, so I don't know
What his eyes might have told me;
But his heavy pace, wearing all he had –
Cast-offs, he remained an incongruous
Interruption to a callous flow
Of well-clad office goers, through whom
He never stopped walking.

I have come upon him, determinedly skirting St. Giles,
I have passed him in front of the National Library,
Glimpsed him traversing the Meadows
Trudging with intent –
And on dark winter afternoons, I have seen him
Heading palacewards, nothing changed
About his person, except a heavier tread
Bowed down with more plastic bags
Added to his collection of worldly possessions.

Yet again ...

I have often squatted on the edge
of Queen Margaret's Loch
stretching my hand out to a swan
spinning round to face me,
its neck a question mark,
its eyes gleaming with expectation,
asking 'have you brought anything?'

And I have drawn my hand back,
feeling guilty, put on the spot
for having rushed out yet another time
with the plastic bag of crumbs
on the bureau in the hall –

venturing on a mission
without the props
that would have spelt success.

As I am Carried from Edinburgh to London

The mist is master here
It manoeuvres the golfer off the links
Making his mortified dog
Sniff behind, as he stops for a drink,

The mist is manipulative,
It teases the lone motorboat
As it speeds down the river
And loses the lady marooned on the road.

The mist is amazing –
It has Machiavellian finesse
Settling on windows of this
Speeding train's prowess

Mooring itself around me –
Forcing me to reason
That it only shrouds a sea
And will lift in London.

London

Nothing seems new, nothing.
I have been here before and everywhere I turn
are traces of yesterday.
As I pause before the British Museum I realise
      I took a picture of St. Paul's
With a cover on my lens – but what of it?
It lives and has lived with me
Through incohesive years, a coherent picture and
          one of many pictures.

I lose my way many a time
Looking for the Underground to take me away from it all
But each time I come back to gaze at another aspect
      of the Tower and
Watch the Tower Bridge gain a new dimension
Standing at a different angle at every fresh encounter ...

I did not lose my way again but had to find it as
Every person I spoke to urged me forward
To where they were all waiting for the guards to change
They did, or so they said
But there they were, as they had been, the past
Telescoped into the present
And as I turned it the wrong way round I saw them
As they would be, only remoter in futurity and smaller
And then it was a decisive goal to capture fragments
      of the Houses

Braving a wind that blew unhindered over the Thames
                              across Westminster Bridge,
That threatened to tear away a mind bent on glueing
                              bits of time together –
The past, the now and the hereafter.
It was a treat – and I knew it
As I saw the softened lights on the Christmas tree
Beyond two smiling policemen at that forbidden door ...

But they were afraid – of me? Oh what an irony!
At least the pigeons know the truth
I am no stranger, and they know it
They eat out of my hand.
What though the fountains are dry?
I can come back again and find solace in the living
And ignore those which speak of artifice
                              in their stony silence.

Between my Two Worlds

When I left London
I wrote of English summers
Of bluebells and blackbirds
And dreamt of the snow.

I came back to Scotland
And longed for the monsoons
The flocks flying homewards
In the deep sunset glow.

My mother's concern, my father's care,
My daughter's soft body that wasn't there;
So I switched my priorities and went back to stay
Carrying deep longings when I went away

To be enfolded in India
In its rich living spree
Yet turning to Britain
In my memory;

Till the unexpected happened
And my worlds switched again
To experience long daylight
And pine for the rain

Of a country burning
With the sun and my pain
Of living between two worlds
That I cannot maintain.

While my mother falters
And my father grows old
I hold *this* my country
As my daughter holds.

The Affirmation

We were late for church, having struggled
To get our daughter out of bed
On a Sunday morning, which is not an easy task.
And we couldn't pretend that we were casual
Visitors, having lost our way. So instead
Of sauntering through the imposing oak archway
We followed our friend, not daring to ask
Her why she led us on this circuitous route
Round this ivy-straddled edifice, scuttling like freed
Chickens to the closed back door –
To slip us in unnoticed, as she had no doubt
That the congregation's concentration would indeed
Be turned to the minister entering the main door.

We were relieved that we'd made it before
The baptism family was summoned to the fore –
But one kindly lady at the end of our pew
In warm Scottish fashion, turned round to show
Her welcome. As she shook hands, she ventured
'And where are you from?' I answered
'We live here' – indicating somewhere close by,
'Where are you actually from?' she repeated urgently.
The priest began the service. I heard the pride
In my voice as I said 'from India'
Which reassured her; but sparks appeared
In my daughter's eyes – dark and protesting
Drowning my explanation, as they explicitly affirmed
That she was from *here* and not just there.

The Kathak Dancers at the Edinburgh Festival

They stand with their backs to you –
These five in black and red.
They do not come to mesmerise you
With their violet silks or golden muslin.

They come in colours you will recognise
And rhythms that will knock you out
Of your complacence, to be startled by
Their intricacies, their daring, their power.

They count, flicking fingers in this
Bated silence. They turn and strike
Deep in your hearts, setting them beating.

They swirl with abandon, rotating and
Revolving till your head reels
And you lose consciousness
Of differences between east and west
And you don't know that you have stood up
And joined in the deafening applause.

Othello in Black and White

Was this *Othello*?
These dancers in black
Standing with their backs
To us ... *Ta dhit-ta - ta-dhit-ta –*
Practising like a graceful
Army ... *Ta-Dha*!
They had turned round –
A mixed cast – from
The East and West.
They told the inside
Story – a play within
A play – the tensions
Between the acts.
The one white man
Not getting the main
Role – then playing
Iago with a vengeance.
The provincial man
With little English
Cast as Othello
– The lead man!
And he doing the
Unbelievable – falling
In love in truth
With the lead lady
The fair Desdemona –
No, not white, but
A Parsi from India!
The English lines
Wouldn't come to life
On Othello's unwilling
Tongue, until he broke
Into his native Assamese,
And played the black man
With conviction and ease.

Dussehra on Calton Hill

While Edinburgh ruminates on a clear Autumn afternoon
A concourse converges on the generous expanse
Of the summit of Calton Hill. The vision is unclouded
With the city reaching out to the Forth, gazing wistfully
At Fife. And caught at the edge of the cliff
Is the startling trio, splashed lovingly
With the colours a hundred children strove to
Clothe them with. While the crowd
Waits mesmerised by Ravana, Kumbhakarna
And Meghnad – the awesome figures of the ancient epics
Stand transformed into these harmless moulds –
Gigantic, Mughal-coated, turbaned or crowned,
Driven to the edge of a Scottish experience
Unwilling to be hurtled down to the estuary –
They stand with amazed expressions, confronting
This western audience, who wait for the
Towering Ravana to be kindled, then his
Brother and his son, reversing the order of
The great Lankan battle, subverting the
History of Empire, as the East travels
To the West and explodes in stars
And streams of fire: the demons of darkness
Destroyed not in battle but amidst
The festivity of people who
Unite to celebrate the Festival
Of Lights, presided over by
The Old Observatory, setting aglow
Nelson's Monument and the forgotten Folly
As a chain in history is brought full circle
To greet the millennium and a new year.

Ripples of Rhythms in Ullapool

The posters were all over the village –
– On the glass of the tourist office
Promising meetings with seals
– At the butchers and bakers
– In the pubs – but not in the churches.
Was it because they innocently
Depicted a god – Nataraj – with four hands
– The still centre shown out of context,
Lifted out of his circle of flames, looking naked
To eyes unused to the invisible layers of
Muslin that clothed Shiva in ancient temples?
There was a fear that they were probably
Denouncing the performers from the
Sunday pulpits, unaware of the
Music that would fold round the
Participants and bring together the
Rhythm of verse and melody
As the god of destruction awoke
From his drugged stupor and descended
To shatter the pace of a tranquil place.

Durga in the North[41]

In heaven the Gods reign –
Bramha, the Lord of Creation,
Vishnu, who indulges the world
To go on under his supervision
As he lies on his lotus, supine.
Her Lord sits, wrapped in lofty
Meditation, above mundane concerns.
She has played the perfect consort –
The adoring, curvaceous Parvati
For artists to carve in admiration
On stone temple walls, a deity
Who stands in suppliant devotion
To one, who in abstemious withdrawal
Takes her charm for granted
Without any open avowal
Of her hypnotic hold on him –
In true Indian style. She is his wife
Who, he knows, has no preference
But to serve his every whim
In sympathetic deference
Through their eternal life.
But she is a mother too
Impatient to resume
Her destined role
Of the powerful creator
Who, in her person, subsumes
The celestial trinity
As Durga, the Mother Goddess.
She has done her duty

---

[41] Durga with her four children was made last October at the National Museum of
Scotland

Of being the beloved
Of a dreaming husband.
She is tired of posturing and assuming
Alluring poses for the benefit
Of one who stores up his
Virile energy for his dance
Of destruction, lost for the time-being
In the fumes of a tantric trance.

So she tells her foursome brood
To have their carriers lined
For the journey down the river
In answer to mankind's
Prayer, who wait every year
For her homecoming
As the daughter of the earth.
Ganesh's mouse gets ready
With ironic mirth
To bear the elephant-headed
To his mundane hearth.
Kartik's regal charioteer
Looks on in peacock pride
Resplendent in its glory –
Fanned out for the ride.
It's colourful exhibition
Is sobered by contrast
To Saraswati's swan
Sailing in full mast,
Watched by the wise
Eyes of Lakshmi's gentle owl
Plain and brown but willing
To let others steal the show.

They come together, gathering
At the mighty source
Of Ganga's knotted journey
From those icy caves,
Awaiting Mother Durga
To lead them down its course.
She comes astride her lion and waves
Them to follow her. On the way
She explains that after their five days
In Bengal's shamianas and homes
They will not return to their heavenly abode.

Instead, they will wend their way
To the North, to be made from Scottish clay,
Softened by Ganga's loam, liberalised
By the dust from the doorstep
Of a prostitute's home, acclimatised
With artificial heat and brought to shape –
Moulded on the brittle frame of barley hay.

They are fashioned by craftsmen
From Krishnanagar's fold
Who bring to life an old
Art in a new domain
Breathing life into Durga
With the final painting
Of her pupil, which makes the figure
Of the ten-armed Goddess
Come alive, ready to bless
At her new destination –
This fresh recruit of a
Scottish congregation.

And while her children
Look on with disbelief
On a scene not rent
With pounding drums
Or chanting priests
Spraying blossoms –
The mouse, has sneaked
With mischievous intent
To Durga's mighty lion
To understand the portent.
The peacock smugly tells
The swan, it is not long
Before they leave this hall
Of artefacts and its throng.
The swan in gracious courtesy
Bends its head and waits.

But owl's sharp eyes
Have followed mouse's tracks
Watching him scamper
Across the floor and back.
So tiny little mouse
In self-important state
Breaks the startling news
To his feathered mates –   ,
That they will not return
To Kailash's misty heights
Or ever watch the dawn
From Indrapuri's gates.
Durga has decided
That as the only one
Having appeared to challenge
The northern sun
She will stay and hold sway
As Mother, won
To her new role –

Never to repeat
Her duties as consort
To a dreamer who dreams on
In his retreat –
Of her return.[42]

---

[42] After Durga Puja (ceremonial worship) she with her children are immersed in a river, symbolic of the journey upstream to Mount Kailash where Shiva waits. The Scottish Durga remains.

From Geddes' West Port Gardens

I have watched the waves of change
Transform this corner of my world
Through the decades, from when I was reclaimed
To be terraced and tended and turned
Into a haven of breathing space and growing life.
I have seen the smoke darkened tenements
Of the Grassmarket lightening their facade
To bring new dignity and hope to their inhabitants.
And when I felt trapped, I could glance
At an angle to revel in the delightful interplay
Of imaginative architecture
Where my creator Geddes had full play
Of his life-infusing skills. Its gleaming white,
Many turreted and towered skyline
Challenging the solid equanimity of the castle,
Which lies across the straight line
Of my vision and my daydreams.

I linger under the flickering shade
Of my chestnut and arching birches,
Inhaling the subtle flavour of rosemary,
Overrun by fern and wild shoots thriving unaided
Today. I lie empty and vacant, my somnolence
Broken only by the jolly bagpipers
Of boy scouts who march up my prominence
While I wait for the People to leave
Their Work and find a Place
Of rest and revival in a regenerated
Ambience of my offered space.

The Moving Image

A city is your city when it
Does not look for a
Camera round your neck
And expect you to stand
Map in hand, undecided
On the kerb, with a faltering
Smile – an island – avoiding which
Its populace flows unconcerned.

A city is your city when it
Does not view you
As a curious interloper
Indulging your sense of indirection
Assuming you have lost your way
Having strayed beyond your
Confines, tolerated temporarily
As an ephemeral guest.

A city is your city when it
Leaves a space for you
In its moving image and
Invites you to step in line
With its unfolding storyline
Mingling, moulding, mirroring
Its myriad dreams
Enhancing vibrant pluralism.

Always ...
to Neil

In the winter of wedding white
When the Castle catches furtive flakes through history
And robins bounce in sight
Hurl your ski-boards down the slope
                   and walk with me.

In the dreamy days of drifting fog
When the Meadows' green horizon melts in mystery
Around the lost, whining dog
Rein in your steed, halt in your tracks
                   and stand by me.

In the afterglow of sunset
When the Forth reaches lazily to greet the sea
And seagulls drift home spent
Turn your yacht, touch prow to shore
                   and come to me.

In the passion of autumnal red
When the Pentlands set their wine wind free
And sheep stand in the gorse amazed
Whirl your steering wheel to veer homeward
                   and stay with me.

Afterword

MANY PEOPLE HAVE asked me why I write only in English and not in my mother tongue, which is Bengali. My answer to them is that I started writing when I came to London as a little girl, in the language I knew – and that was English. So English became the language of creative expression for me, in which I spoke and dreamt for a long time thereafter. I guess children learn as quickly as they forget, and that is what happened with me. I picked up English and forgot Bengali. But after I went back to India, I learnt Bengali with the same amazing speed, but as there was no language support system in Indian schools in those days, there was no one to help me to master the literary Bengali which one needs to write in it with confidence. Moreover, I went to a very British boarding school (probably more British than schools in Britain) up in the Himalayas, where we weren't allowed to indulge in the rich vernaculars of the Indian nation (though we did in secret and private conversations). So English remained my sole tool to wield as I pleased, in verse.

For a long time I was embarrassed about writing in English. Since I had started writing just before I turned seven, a lot of my early poetry is pretty awful, valued only by my parents who have lovingly kept the piles of notebooks of bad verse, which I shudder to own. But when you are young, you are unselfconscious and I happily entered competitions, winning prizes like the Commonwealth Scholar Prize, the Statesman and Junior Statesman Prizes, etc. for poetry. Then there was the criticism of writing in a 'foreign language' and a period when poetry was considered 'unfashionable'. So there were years when I kept my writing largely to myself, except for some very close friends, and of course, my faithful, encouraging parents, to whom I *had* to read every poem I wrote and seek their approval. I must say that without their unfailing support I would not have continued writing and valuing poetry. If I had relied only on their judgement, I would have had a very uncritical audience who invariably met every poem of mine with the unflagging response 'that is very good'!

As an adult, I was shy about publishing. I wasn't sure about how my poetry would be received. I didn't even know whether it was good or bad! Funny that, as I had studied English Literature at University, doing Honours and Masters in it and taught it at University, and could identify and enjoy good poetry! But my secret love with my first love, i.e. poetry, continued. It was when I was in Edinburgh University, working on my PhD where I was free to attend lectures and tutorials, that my perspective changed. One of my tutors Mimo Caenapeel, in her unabashed love of poetry, sharing her enthusiastic appreciation of verse with us, made me realise that I needn't tuck this love affair of mine away like a guilty secret. I then felt justified in loving poetry for what it was – rhythmic, a clever play on language, inviting the most outrageous games with sound patterns, its multiple layers of meaning appropriate to carry political messages and confidential emotions for the lover of poetry to uncover at will. So that was when I went back to teaching poetry with gusto and writing it with a sense of urgency. It was my therapeutic medium.

What did I write about? Of course I wrote about my British experience for a while, of 'bluebells and blackbirds', of English summers and London! I spent my schooldays on the beautifully exhilarating Himalayas and my holidays on the foothills, against their majestic backdrop – this time on a University campus. It was a humbling experience, living on and beside the towering might of the highest mountain range in the world with its dense forest and vegetation and distant snow peaks! We were indulged in our convent school, breaking all possible rules, threatened with expulsion which never materialised. On the campus, we picnicked in the sal forest, waded in the local river and caught fish which we set free immediately after, read voraciously, borrowing from a wonderful library, precociously attended University seminars and organized dance dramas, musicals and plays which we staged with enthusiasm. So I wrote about the Himalayas and of the freedom we enjoyed.

At university we were caught in the extremist Naxalite movement. Those were turbulent political times. A generation of youth in Bengal was simply picked up by police vans and made to disappear. We thought we could change the world. But my parents had other plans to see me live and not die in jail. So they transferred me from Presidency College, the hotbed of politics to Lady Brabourne College, where I was the General Secretary of the Students' Union, but it was safely, 'apolitical'! That did not stop my poems from being political or feminist. I did get published in our College Literary magazine, but in general, my poetry remained my personal safety valve, more so when I had a disastrous first marriage. It was my lifeline to sanity, inspired by my delicate, frightened little daughter.

So when did the private become public? A friend, Anjan Datta, made me fill in forms for two successive years and made me give him some of the poems for the Poetry Society (India) Anthologies, brought out by the British Council. They were published. But I retreated again. I was fighting a draining and painful legal battle to obtain my daughter's full custody. The irony was that she was always with me, but could be taken away unless the court 'granted' me the right to keep her. I fought back like a tigress and my poetry in this period is full of anger and pain. In fact, I find that I usually write when I am angry or sad, and very seldom when I am happy.

Meeting Neil changed everything for me. When my daughter wanted

'Uncle Neil' as her father, I gave up my fierce feminist independence, realising that there were some good men in the world after all, for whom it was worthwhile giving up a full-time, permanent university teaching job, my parents and country and follow him to Scotland, where I had studied a few years back. And I now know that my two countries have always lived with me, as I miss the other and defend it when I am away.

And it is in Scotland that I found friends who introduced me to a whole world of writers where poetry seems to come as easily as leaves to a tree! Every poet needs at least one person to believe in her/his work. That person for me in Scotland was Angus Calder, who introduced me to Sally Evans and Ian King of Diehard, who were very brave to publish an Indo-Scot whom no-one had heard of. That was the breakthrough I needed. I continued publishing in anthologies, magazines and newspapers, and my poetry piled up, enough for two more volumes, screaming to see the daylight of print. But poetry publishers are few and far between and funding is scarce. I felt desperately shelved. Writing can be a lonely thing. But I continued writing. The piles of rejections were always higher than the acceptances. But there were people like John Hudson, Elaine Greig, Tom Bryan, Alec Finlay, Stuart Campbell, Liz Niven, Elspeth Brown, Joy Hendry, Colin Will and others, who remained a source of encouragement, though there were times when I did suffer from intense moments of depression. And the most constant force that kept me going was Neil's faith in my work.

One gentle writer friend whose work I value and admire, read my work and sustained my motivation to keep writing. That was Alan Jamieson. Then I heard of the path-breaking work Luath Press was doing. I agonised over 'to send or not to send' my poetry to Gavin MacDougall. In the end, Neil did. Their books are beautifully laid out and they have published the work of poets I admire. So when Gavin said Luath Press would publish my poetry, I felt as if I was flying over the Himalayas and seeing sunrise on those peaks again. This is my new dawn. And when I timidly asked Alan to edit and write the introduction to this volume, I was overjoyed when he readily agreed. The title was suggested by Gavin, with the careless grace of a master conjuror, who finds the appropriate title at the drop of a hat! I couldn't have chosen a better one to combine my two countries, living in one and dreaming of another in a language which *is* mine because I write in it.

Bashabi Fraser

Some other books published by **LUATH** PRESS

POETRY

Drink the Green Fairy
Brian Whittingham
ISBN 1 84282 020 6 PB £8.99

The Ruba'iyat of Omar Khayyam, in Scots
Rab Wilson
ISBN 1 84282 046 X PB £8.99

Talking with Tongues
Brian Finch
ISBN 1 84282 006 0 PB £8.99

Kate o Shanter's Tale and other poems [book]
Matthew Fitt
ISBN 1 84282 028 1 PB £6.99

Kate o Shanter's Tale and other poems [audio CD]
Matthew Fitt
ISBN 1 84282 043 5 PB £9.99

Bad Ass Raindrop
Kokumo Rocks
ISBN 1 84282 018 4 PB £6.99

Madame Fifi's Farewell and other poems
Gerry Cambridge
ISBN 1 84282 005 2 PB £8.99

Picking Brambles
Des Dillon
ISBN 1 84282 021 4 PB £6.99

Sex, Death & Football
Alistair Findlay
ISBN 1 84282 022 2 PB £6.99

Poems to be Read Aloud
introduced by Tom Atkinson
ISBN 0 946487 00 6 PB £5.00

Scots Poems to be Read Aloud
intro Stuart McHardy
ISBN 0 946487 81 2 PB £5.00

The Luath Burns Companion
John Cairney
ISBN 1 84282 000 1 PB £10.00

Immortal Memories: A Compilation of Toasts to the Memory of Burns as delivered at Burns Suppers, 1801-2001
John Cairney
ISBN 1 84282 009 5 HB £20.00

Blind Harry's Wallace
Hamilton of Gilbertfield
introduced and edited by Elspeth King
ISBN 0 946487 33 2 PB £8.99

The Whisky Muse: Scotch whisky in poem & song
Robin Laing
ISBN 1 84282 041 9 PB £7.99

FICTION

Driftnet
Lin Anderson
ISBN 1 84282 034 6 PB £9.99

The Fundamentals of New Caledonia
David Nicol
ISBN 1 84282 93 6 HB £16.99

Milk Treading
Nick Smith
ISBN 1 84282 037 0 PB £6.99

The Road Dance
John MacKay
ISBN 1 84282 024 9 PB £9.99

The Strange Case of RL Stevenson
Richard Woodhead
ISBN 0 946487 86 3 HB £16.99

But n Ben A-Go-Go
Matthew Fitt
ISBN 0 946487 82 0 HB £10.99
ISBN 1 84282 014 1 PB £6.99

The Bannockburn Years
William Scott
ISBN 0 946487 34 0 PB £7.95

The Great Melnikov
Hugh MacLachlan
ISBN 0 946487 42 1 PB £7.95

FOLKLORE

Scotland: Myth, Legend & Folklore
Stuart McHardy
ISBN 0 946487 69 3 PB £7.99

Luath Storyteller: Highland Myths & Legends
George W Macpherson
ISBN 1 84282 003 6 PB £5.00

Tales of the North Coast
Alan Temperley
ISBN 0 946487 18 9 PB £8.99

Tall Tales from an Island
Peter Macnab
ISBN 0 946487 07 3 PB £8.99

The Supernatural Highlands
Francis Thompson
ISBN 0 946487 31 6 PB £8.99

CARTOONS

Broomie Law
Cinders McLeod
ISBN 0 946487 99 5 PB £4.00

THE QUEST FOR

The Quest for Robert Louis Stevenson
John Cairney
ISBN 0 946487 87 1 HB £16.99

The Quest for the Nine Maidens
Stuart McHardy
ISBN 0 946487 66 9 HB £16.99

The Quest for the Original Horse Whisperers
Russell Lyon
ISBN 1 842820 020 6 HB £16.99

The Quest for the Celtic Key
Karen Ralls-MacLeod and
Ian Robertson
ISBN 1 842820 031 1 PB £8.99

The Quest for Arthur
Stuart McHardy
ISBN 1 842820 12 5 HB £16.99

ON THE TRAIL OF

On the Trail of William Wallace
David R Ross
ISBN 0 946487 47 2 PB £7.99

On the Trail of Robert the Bruce
David R Ross
ISBN 0 946487 52 9 PB £7.99

On the Trail of Mary Queen of Scots
J Keith Cheetham
ISBN 0 946487 50 2 PB £7.99

On the Trail of Bonnie Prince Charlie
David R Ross
ISBN 0 946487 68 5 PB £7.99

On the Trail of Robert Burns
John Cairney
ISBN 0 946487 51 0 PB £7.99

On the Trail of John Muir
Cherry Good
ISBN 0 946487 62 6 PB £7.99

On the Trail of Queen Victoria in the Highlands
Ian R Mitchell
ISBN 0 946487 79 0 PB £7.99

On the Trail of Robert Service
G Wallace Lockhart
ISBN 0 946487 24 3 PB £7.99

On the Trail of the Pilgrim Fathers
J Keith Cheetham
ISBN 0 946487 83 9 PB £7.99

LUATH GUIDES TO SCOTLAND

The North West Highlands: Roads to the Isles
Tom Atkinson
ISBN 0 946487 54 5 PB £4.95

Mull and Iona: Highways and Byways
Peter Macnab
ISBN 0 946487 58 8 PB £4.95

The Northern Highlands: The Empty Lands
Tom Atkinson
ISBN 0 946487 55 3 PB £4.95

The West Highlands: The Lonely Lands
Tom Atkinson
ISBN 0 946487 56 1 PB £4.95

HISTORY

Scots in Canada
Jenni Calder
ISBN 1 84282 038 9 PB £7.99

Civil Warrior
Robin Bell
ISBN 1 84282 013 3 HB £10.99

A Passion for Scotland
David R Ross
ISBN 1 84282 019 2 PB £5.99

Reportage Scotland
Louise Yeoman
ISBN 0 946487 61 8 PB £9.99

Plaids & Bandanas: Highland Drover to Wild West Cowboy
Rob Gibson
ISBN 0 946487 88 X PB £7.99

POLITICS & CURRENT ISSUES

Scotlands of the Mind
Angus Calder
ISBN 1 84282 008 7 PB £9.99

Trident on Trial: the case for people's disarmament
Angie Zelter
ISBN 1 84282 004 4 PB £9.99

Uncomfortably Numb: A Prison Requiem
Maureen Maguire
ISBN 1 84282 001 X PB £8.99

Scotland: Land & Power – Agenda for Land Reform
Andy Wightman
ISBN 0 946487 70 7 PB £5.00

Old Scotland New Scotland
Jeff Fallow
ISBN 0 946487 40 5 PB £6.99

Some Assembly Required: behind the scenes at the rebirth of the Scottish Parliament
David Shepherd
ISBN 0 946487 84 7 PB £7.99

Notes from the North
Emma Wood
ISBN 0 946487 46 4 PB £8.99

NATURAL WORLD

The Hydro Boys: pioneers of renewable energy
Emma Wood
ISBN 1 84282 016 8 HB £16.99

Wild Scotland
James McCarthy
ISBN 0 946487 37 5 PB £8.99

Wild Lives: Otters – On the Swirl of the Tide
Bridget MacCaskill
ISBN 0 946487 67 7 PB £9.99

Wild Lives: Foxes – The Blood is Wild
Bridget MacCaskill
ISBN 0 946487 71 5 PB £9.99

Scotland – Land & People: An Inhabited Solitude
James McCarthy
ISBN 0 946487 57 X PB £7.99

The Highland Geology Trail
John L Roberts
ISBN 0 946487 36 7 PB £4.99

Red Sky at Night
John Barrington
ISBN 0 946487 60 X PB £8.99

Listen to the Trees
Don MacCaskill
ISBN 0 946487 65 0 PB £9.99

WALK WITH LUATH

Skye 360: walking the coastline of Skye
Andrew Dempster
ISBN 0 946487 85 5 PB £8.99

Walks in the Cairngorms
Ernest Cross
ISBN 0 946487 09 X PB £4.95

Short Walks in the Cairngorms
Ernest Cross
ISBN 0 946487 23 5 PB £4.95

The Joy of Hillwalking
Ralph Storer
ISBN 0 946487 28 6 PB £7.50

Scotland's Mountains before the Mountaineers
Ian R Mitchell
ISBN 0 946487 39 1 PB £9.99

Mountain Days and Bothy Nights
Dave Brown and Ian R Mitchell
ISBN 0 946487 15 4 PB £7.50

SPORT

Ski & Snowboard Scotland
Hilary Parke
ISBN 0 946487 35 9 PB £6.99

Over the Top with the Tartan Army
Andy McArthur
ISBN 0 946487 45 6 PB £7.99

SOCIAL HISTORY

Pumpherston: the story of a shale oil village
Sybil Cavanagh
ISBN 1 84282 011 7 HB £17.99
ISBN 1 84282 015 X PB £10.99

Shale Voices
Alistair Findlay
ISBN 0 946487 78 2 HB £17.99
ISBN 0 946487 48 0 PB £10.99

A Word for Scotland
Jack Campbell
ISBN 0 946487 48 0 PB £12.99

TRAVEL & LEISURE

**Die Kleine Schottlandfibel
[Scotland Guide in German]**
Hans-Walter Arends
ISBN 0 946487 89 8 PB £8.99

Let's Explore Edinburgh Old Town
Anne Bruce English
ISBN 0 946487 98 7 PB £4.99

Edinburgh's Historic Mile
Duncan Priddle
ISBN 0 946487 97 9 PB £2.99

**Pilgrims in the Rough: St Andrews
beyond the 19th hole**
Michael Tobert
ISBN 0 946487 74 X PB £7.99

LANGUAGE

**Luath Scots Language Learner
[Book]**
L Colin Wilson
ISBN 0 946487 91 X PB £9.99

**Luath Scots Language Learner
[Double Audio CD Set]**
L Colin Wilson
ISBN 1 84282 026 5 CD £16.99

FOOD & DRINK

**First Foods Fast: how to prepare
good simple meals for your baby**
Lara Boyd
ISBN 1 84282 002 8 PB £4.99

Edinburgh and Leith Pub Guide
Stuart McHardy
ISBN 0 946487 80 4 PB £4.95

BIOGRAPHY

The Last Lighthouse
Sharma Krauskopf
ISBN 0 946487 96 0 PB £7.99

Tobermory Teuchter
Peter Macnab
ISBN 0 946487 41 3 PB £7.99

Bare Feet and Tackety Boots
Archie Cameron
ISBN 0 946487 17 0 PB £7.95

Come Dungeons Dark
John Taylor Caldwell
ISBN 0 946487 19 7 PB £6.95

GENEALOGY

**Scottish Roots: step-by-step
guide for ancestor hunters**
Alwyn James
ISBN 1 84282 007 9 PB £9.99

WEDDINGS, MUSIC AND DANCE

The Scottish Wedding Book
G Wallace Lockhart
ISBN 1 94282 010 9 PB £12.99

Fiddles and Folk
G Wallace Lockhart
ISBN 0 946487 38 3 PB £7.95

Highland Balls and Village Halls
G Wallace Lockhart
ISBN 0 946487 12 X PB £6.95

Luath Press Limited
committed to publishing well written books worth reading

LUATH PRESS takes its name from Robert Burns, whose little collie Luath (*Gael.*, swift or nimble) tripped up Jean Armour at a wedding and gave him the chance to speak to the woman who was to be his wife and the abiding love of his life. Burns called one of *The Twa Dogs* Luath after Cuchullin's hunting dog in *Ossian's Fingal*. Luath Press was established in 1981 in the heart of Burns country, and is now based a few steps up the road from Burns' first lodgings on Edinburgh's Royal Mile. Luath offers you distinctive writing with a hint of unexpected pleasures.

Most bookshops in the UK, the US, Canada, Australia, New Zealand and parts of Europe either carry our books in stock or can order them for you. To order direct from us, please send a £sterling cheque, postal order, international money order or your credit card details (number, address of cardholder and expiry date) to us at the address below. Please add post and packing as follows: UK – £1.00 per delivery address; overseas surface mail – £2.50 per delivery address; overseas airmail – £3.50 for the first book to each delivery address, plus £1.00 for each additional book by airmail to the same address. If your order is a gift, we will happily enclose your card or message at no extra charge.

Luath Press Limited
543/2 Castlehill
The Royal Mile
Edinburgh EH1 2ND
Scotland
Telephone: 0131 225 4326 (24 hours)
Fax: 0131 225 4324
email: gavin.macdougall@luath.co.uk
Website: www.luath.co.uk